D1496358

AIR POCKET

AIR POCKET

KIMIKO HAHN

Hanging Loose Press

Published by Hanging Loose Press
231 Wyckoff Street
Brooklyn, New York 11217

The publisher gratefully acknowledges grants from the
Literature Programs of the National Endowment for the Arts
and the New York State Council on the Arts in support of the
publication of this book.

Cover art by Tomie Arai

Acknowledgments: Some of these poems first appeared in *The
Agni Review, Appeal to Reason, Blind Alleys, Bridge: Asian
American Perspectives, Columbia: A Magazine of Poetry and
Prose, Contact II, Hanging Loose, Heresies, Ikon, The South
Dakota Review, The Washington Review,* and *Breaking Silence:
An Anthology of Contemporary Asian American Poetry*
(Greenfield Review Press, 1983)

Library   of   Congress   Cataloging-in-Publication   Data
Hahn, Kimiko, 1955-
        Air pocket / Kimiko Hahn.
            p.   cm.
        ISBN 0-914610-52-X   — ISBN 0-914610-51-1 (pbk.)
        I. Title.
        PS3558.A32357A74   1988
811'.54 — dc19   88-39629
                                                        CIP

Produced at The Print Center., Inc., 225 Varick St.,
New York, NY 10014, a non-profit facility for literary
and arts-related publications. (212) 206-8465

CONTENTS

for my mother and father

But the Parsee came down from his palm tree,
wearing his hat, from which the rays of the
sun were reflected in more-than-oriental
splendour, packed up his cooking-stove, and
went away in the direction of Orotavo, Amygdala,
the Upland Meadows of Anantarivo, and the
Marshes of Sonaput.

"How the Rhinoceros Got His Skin"
Rudyard Kipling

WHEN YOU LEAVE

This sadness could only be a color
if we call it *momoiro,* Japanese

for *peach-color,* as in the first story
Mother told us: It is the color of the hero's skin

when the barren woman discovered him
inside a peach floating down the river.

And of the banner and gloves she sewed
when he left her to battle the horsemen, then found himself

torn, like fruit off a tree. Even when he met a monkey
dog and bird he could not release

the color he saw when he closed his eyes.
        In his boat
the lap of the waves against the hold

was too intimate as he leaned back to sleep.
        He wanted
to leave all thoughts of peach behind him —

the fruit that brought him to her
and she, the one who opened the color forever.

DANCE INSTRUCTIONS FOR A YOUNG GIRL

Stand: knees slightly
bent, toes in *posed*
you watch the hawk over the river
curve, until his voice, shoulders back
gently *overcome by Seiji's mouth*
against yours, the white breath, and elbows
close to your side. *The silk cords*
and sash crush your lungs you are
young — beautiful, and almost
elegant. The layers of cloth pastel,
bright red and moist,
twist around. Follow his flow
of steps, a shallow stream between rocks
the carp. Seiji draws your hand
toward him or a stroke.
Before you look back turn your chin
in a figure eight, tilt, balance
then kneel quickly *the relief of cloth*
pulled off. Bow to him and the audience.
When you straighten, his black and red lines
against the white powder
are drawn, as his gesture
and step, perfectly. More perfectly *the weight*
of his chest than your own, although his
belongs to you, a woman.

Note: geisha were traditionally told to imitate female impersonator Kabuki actors.

BON ODORI

Nothing eats the kimonos
in the trunk
under the stairs. We save them.
And sometimes I think 'mulberry'
or 'cocoons.' They were grandmother's;
none for weddings, all
for dance, the sleeves fall below
our waists. I do not see
Utamaro's woman,
paper in her teeth—not his
woodcut, rather Cassatt's drypoint,
The Letter: her head, black
hair tied back, bent forward
as she licks the envelope,
exactly like you, mother.
On that July night
we will see the New Jersey Palisades
but first we'll go to temple,
clap twice in front of all those boxes,
light incense. In winter we write
about summer. We send letters: the silk
the color of raw tuna, and its water pattern,
tie-dyed shapes like fish eggs,
will look well in the circle
of dancers. The drummer
is always so handsome! Sleeves
and moths flutter and
lanterns sway in the heat. The drummer,
half naked, is in the center.

ROOST

The cane fields blaze
into a black glow
until the smoke
covers us
and grandmother's voice
downstairs wakes me.
She sets steaming rice
before grandfather's photo
in the lacquer shrine
while the rooster
lets the morning out
of his throat.

As I shuffle
through feathers and mangoes
she asks, *the 'tori'*
woke you? then
is 'tori' English?
When I laugh
she laughs.
I shake my head
and remember her voice
like the roost
in the backyard.

Later she guesses
it's Japanese. It's
'chicken.' And when we bathe
she laughs again.
The steam rises from her back
and breasts. The laughter
fills every corner
and the lizards fill
the screen.

Tomorrow we pile
all the rotting fruit?
She nods. The lacquer doors
close, the flies on the mango
rest until daylight
and her hands
cover her stomach.
As I fall back
on her enormous bed
her words are muffled,
scratching their way
through ashes and air.

TEETH

The leaf and fruit shade spotted on his skin
exaggerates his age, the large brown spaces
moving on arms, knees and forehead.
He needs you. You wheel his chair across the yard,
chickens parting, towards the porch
where grandmother and father play cards.
Matches are gambled until supper.
You leave grandfather and arrange five plates.
He places his teeth in a water glass.
You laugh. And everyone else laughs at you
except grandfather: he cries and mother explains
he is laughing also. Now in this midwestern winter
the heat from the radiator waves a curtain
in your own apartment. You feel
the novel in your lap is made of bone
and tissue. It concerns an old man
and his daughter-in-law's abortion.
The park they meet in afterwards is filled with pine
and the squash outside her kitchen window
touches the soil, here.

TEA

This bowl
is a pair of cupped hands, yours
given to me.

*   *   *

Repeat the same gesture
Until you hear how quietly the air parts
When your hand reaches for the purple cloth.
This posture speaks
To your neighbor's squalor,

The elegance of this cup's form and color —
How elegant your footstep:
Grandfather left Hiroshima
To burn sugar cane in Maui. But you are here
And after sitting on your knees for an hour

The starched socks separate from your ankles,
Walk over beside the teacher
And watch you rise quickly.
You walk knees bent. Relaxed. The silk
Around your ribs holds your breath.

*   *   *

When you finish put away the charcoal,
iron kettle, scoop, tea — and notice
as you place the bowl inside its box
how hot it feels.

AS THE DOLLS GROW OLDER THE GIRLS CHANGE

from pine cone to spruce,
saucer to cup, etc.
Somewhat different from the dolls
themselves: plastic,
rag, china.

Eat this medicine
and don't let me catch you
spitting it out.
The dolls taught us
everything: squeeze,
slap, kiss, and sass.
This is your last chance.

Some days they talked back.
You couldn't stand it
and shrieked.
I'm your mother for godsake.

Some of the dolls
you could never play with
like the Japanese beauty.
She had a hard time breathing
in the glass box
but got used to it
mother said.
You kept wishing she'd faint
so you could open the door
and pinch her face.

Later came tits and ass —
the doll
you had to ask grandma to buy.
And her miniskirts,

pizzas and Ken.
Wow.
If only he had had a cock
everything
would have worked out
okay.

As the dolls grew older
you gave them
to your little sister.
She happily
stuck them
in her mouth.
You can see her
as you were:
dolls on lap,
offering nipples
from a flat chest.
Talking and humming.

Once you get used to blood
it almost doesn't matter.
It takes all of high school,
linen, skirts.
The dolls had been useless
but at home
you threw yourself on them
and cried *cut it
out cut it out.*
Yet what is your weakness
becomes your strength,
calendar, identity, lawn,
rock garden, pond. Swim in it
baby.

The first mistake you made
was smiling back.

fucking cunt
she'll get hers
and I'll give it
if she tries
one more time
that razor tongue
bitch the nerve
to even look that way
at him

Speaking of razors
reminds you of Sheila
in confirmation class
when she hiked up her skirt
to show you
his initials
scratched across her thigh
and talked about
his tongue in your mouth.
oh jesus
does that mean I'll get
a disease

they lie on top of you
can you imagine

When Eurasian
was definitely exotic
but totally unhip
the dolls meant nothing
but white babies

or animals.
Being nice
was not a priority.
Smashing the Japanese doll
for example.
Shards of glass, splinters,
ceramic head
and hands all over the carpet.
Just a thought.

Still what you desire
has the sensibility of the nursery:
you go from their chest
to your own
to the chest you put them in.

A GIRL COMBS HER HAIR

after Li Ho

Recently cut she is unaccustomed
to the blunt end

just above her moist shoulders.
Even in the morning

the air feels close — closer
than his shirt

slipped over her head.
The comb glides through the luster,

and stops short.
She thinks of fingers. Hands

gripping the small of her back. She leans
against the wall. He could have

brought flowers. The girl wants
to sit for a while on the fire escape:

to listen to the water
draining the open fire hydrant

and cooling the street and children —
to figure out the look he gave

when she turned and small hairs
scattered across the pillow. But already

it's so oppressive. She would collect
all her combs and snap them in half

but a scent keeps her
from moving from the sheets.

By her sandals she notices an orchid
in white tissue. She reaches.

DAUGHTER

Although I'm oldest I can't
be the one who paints

or speaks grandmother's language
like a picture-bride marriage

to a still life: a plate
of oranges, plums and grapes

one takes care to arrange
precise as syntax — as a passage

one must translate
for someone else. That

is the greater danger
than waking with a stranger.

SPRING

I am very happy
lying on this rug
beside the dog, listening
to the constant roar
of spring rain.
Everything I need
is here — even the desire
now drawing me
to the window to recall
the deer wandering
in the city of Nara.
As they gather around me
I feed them cake
from a hand
in my childhood.

LOSS

Morning

I must leave speaking
when I see the black branches
over a roof
or head. In a few hours
this hunger will be removed
and migrations south
south. The only green
is that room.

Evening

Their voices were better than words
or calendars and the nurse
who massaged fingers and calves
was stronger than the man
holding my coat. I forgot
all my questions. Still the branches
knock together constantly. But we can sleep
birds in flight.

IMAGINATION

i.   Mine

He grinds his teeth
in sleep and more often
shouts. Yet not even
the train whistle
below the window
wakes him. It enters
his dream
like a mother
in a black slip.
Through the smoke
the graveyard shift
emerges
like hard moist
roots. Nothing
grows here. The light
teases the fern.
Could another man
move me — when I stand
the room disappears
for a second.

ii. Second

His tanned chest
and white ass
against the sheet
startle me
and I laugh,
my whole body
shaking. I don't even
remember his name
and after he leaves
I spread
the classifieds
on the floor

and begin circling
as though I'd leave today
for half a dozen rooms
in the City
'w/view or sink.'

iii. Sink

I am more alone now
unable to describe
to anyone
the variety of reds
around the room:
the fuchsia, scarlet,
maroon — maroon
as the red
in one's mouth
or as genitals.
But more,
like my clothes
as I open the drawers
to leave.

iv. Leaves

With the bus ticket
in the back
of the cupboard,
the maps
across my lap
cease to comfort.
Before he left
for work
he just massaged
my neck. He found
the empty drawer

and newspaper
clippings. The coffee
has no flavor.
Through the morning glories
and leaves
I watch him
cross the yards.
He can offer
nothing better
than his union contract.
And me —
I run out
to the hedges.

v.   Hedges

He doesn't want me
more than anything else
to follow him
to those shafts
and would never
wait for me
like some dream
of Louisville.
I'll leave it inside
for now. I run
towards the mine,
forgetting the milk
on the counter
and realizing the walls
of that room
are my imagination.

SPONGE

i.   The post card from Frostproof
is taped to the wall
above your desk. It regards you
a tourist as you stare
curiously. In it the man
in the deep sea diving suit
cannot be seen. But you know
he's there in shorts or nude
under all the metal
and air hose. He smiles at you.
You'd like to meet him.
All afternoon
you walk up and down Broadway
searching for one of his dozen
giant sponges.

ii.   It is approximately the size
of your head
and you finally touch it to the water
so it floats above your body
in the bath. From breast to ankle
it travels and with a kind
of satisfaction fills with water again.
You hold it against your skin
and begin to sponge.

iii.   You finally get in touch
and dine together.
"No fish," he requests. Immediately
you like him. You want him
to take off his suit
and stay a while. "Isn't it hot
under all that metal?"
"One acclimates,"
he replies. On the topic
of postcards he's quite proficient
and assumes various strangleholds
against octopus and mermaid alike.

Your body tingles at the thought:
the sun fathoms above, and your diver
with nothing more than metal skin
for safety. Sabotage would be so simple—
a mere splice or pinch! After a little wine
you dance and his helmet
feels hot. Still he won't
take it off and you decide he's just
a sponge.

THE OPERATION

Taking notes
in the amphitheater
you saw him:
his heart framed
by green, white and red.
Recognizing him
years later
at the shore
(the scar
and his eyebrows
that unusual)
he mistook you
for a fiction teacher
he had "scored with
a few times"
until you retold
the jokes
the doctors had
while stitching:
"They made
the operation
memorable."
"Thanks."
He bought
a couple beers
each. Then he left
ten years later
for a yogurt maker.
At the door
he picked a fight
as though you
knew something
no one else could.
Something
that would make others
queasy. "Perhaps
if I had known you

before your operation,"
you tried.
"Perhaps
if I could see
your breast opened
like a personal
letter — "
In reply you grinned
instead of explaining again
about seeing others.
The next week
when you found
his burgundy t-shirt
in the laundry
you got angry finally
and thought
of the sponges
that had glistened
so brightly
you could almost smell
the red. You wonder
if perhaps one wasn't
left inside.

THE AVOCADO

Searching for one perfect avocado you walk
in and out of vegetable stands and *bodegas*
and circle hawkers until you come in contact
with the exact firmness (soft), most brilliant
brightness, tastiest fragrance, shiniest
texture, best price, and of course while
shaking it, that knock from the pit
which has separated from the fruit. At home
however you find your children and dog
grown, the apartment immaculately refurnished,
and your husband remarried, assuming that
during the interval you were either caught
in that fallout accident or you ran off
with some pseudo-socialist religious cult.
Dinner in any case is ready and you're invited
to sit down.

THE GLADIOLAS

At first I wasn't sure
so little was taken
then slowly recognized
his stages of decision:
comb, toothbrush,
styptic pencil, alarm.

I was thinking of deer
when I came home.
At Uncle Ted's farm
among rows of hybrid gladiolas
the deer tore and chewed
leaving behind dark spikes

when the truck pulled up
or until the sun rose.
· I was eight and barely recall
the men working.
Rather the enormous
ragged stalks and deer droppings.

I don't remember
but we saw the deer.
As we turned the bend
their white tails froze
long enough for the men to swear
they'd shoot them.

The faucet was dripping
when I walked in,
a sign he'd been home
and rinsed the coffee cup
now face down
in the dish rack.

THE WOMAN WITH THE SUITCASE

is around every corner
when mother brings us Saturdays

to the Loop. We never look for her
and *must have a soda at Kresge's,*

watching her speak close to mother.
We hear a foreign language: *HUAC*

USSR FBI. She grips the case
between her knees as she touches

mother's arm. The scuff marks
strike me like scars or lace.

Father said, *don't let your imagination
run wild.* She returned home

one evening to find her mailbox
and rooms inside out

and her brother in the kitchen
both knees broken. *Jane,*

be outraged, she said
and left. *Papers, all papers,*

mother shook her head. Across the wall
in her bedroom in letters

the size of a man: R E D

THE AIR ITSELF

The fire hydrants clear
and cool the soft streets.
Arms and legs
cluster in doorsteps:
I am tired.
What have we to see
or sell: teeth,
tongue, fingers, blood.
I own these. I rent three windows
and plumbing.
Strip the walls—is that a neighbor
or water pipes?
The streetlights attract shadows
and paper bags. I am tired.
How many colors mix to make brown,
these buildings? Touch me:
throw the blanket off the bed.
You smell like industrial glue,
vinyl, and sweat. Embrace.
Clutch. I am tired.
Forget trembling and persuade me
to feel: revolt.
Begin now. We are tired.
Gather. The air itself
suffocates this morning.

THE BATH: AUGUST 6, 1945

Bathing the summer night
off my arms and breasts
I heard a plane
overhead *I heard*
the door rattle
froze
then relaxed
in the cool water
one more moment
one private moment
before waking the children
and mother-in-law,
before the heat
before the midday heat
drenched my spirits again.
I had wanted
to also relax
in thoughts of my husband —
how we were children
when he was drafted
imprisoned — but didn't dare
and rose from the tub,
dried off lightly
and slipped on cotton work pants.
Caution drew me to the window
and there an enormous blossom of fire
a hand changed my life
and made the world shiver —
a light that tore flesh
so it slipped off limbs,
swelled so
no one could recognize
a mother or child
a hand that tore the door open
pushed me on the floor
ripped me up —
I will never have children again

so even today
my hair has not grown back
my teeth still shards
and one eye blind
and it would be easy,
satisfying somehow
to write it off as history
those men are there
each time I close
my one good eye
each time or lay blame
on men or militarists
the children cry out
in my sleep
where they still live
for the sake of a night's rest.
But it isn't air raids
simply
that we survive
but *gold worth its weight*
in blood the coal,
oil, uranium we mine
and drill
yet cannot call our own.
And it would be gratifying
to be called a survivor
I am a survivor
since I live if I didn't wonder
about survival today—
at 55, widowed at 18—
if I didn't feel
the same oppressive August heat
auto parts in South Africa,
Mexico, Alabama,
and shiver not from memory
or terror
but anger that this wounded body
must stand *take a stand*

and cry out
as only a newborn baby can cry—
I live, I will live
I will to live
in spite of history
to make history
in my vision of peace—
that morning in the bath
so calm
so much my right
though I cannot return to that moment
I bring these words to you
hoping to hold you
to hold you
and to take hold.

June 12, 1982
New York City

NORA

Other women say other women
gave more than Nora
and she says so also.
The streets, named after martyrs,
are filled with women:
Marta, Bertha, Ariel,
Rita, Beatriz, Arlen, —
and there are compañeras
who can tell you about regiments of men they led
or mothers who joined
in mourning a child's death or rape.
Indeed Nora spent her Saturdays
at the golf course or poolside
at the Country Club
outside her father's cattle ranch.
Her *adoring* father
pushed this little girl
to a vision broader than sink and bed
in the town then Villa Somoza,
in the days when she dreamed of marrying
someone with an aristocratic name.
But she knew the poor also:
visiting the hospitals crowded as slums
and teaching hygiene and religion
in the slums diseased as the hospitals.
She knew even then charities
would not satisfy.
But when she campaigned
for the opposition leader, Aguero,
her parents sent her to the Catholic University,
Washington, DC
and she baked in isolation
from her country's history
and from our own days of massive escalation
and the slaughter of the Vietnamese people
(who would also claim victory in time).
It was, she said, *the two most superficial
years of my life.* 1968

1969
Returning to Managua
Nora entered law school,
believing in justice.
But her lessons revolved around political prisoners
and as my friend, a lawyer, learned,
the law is to *defend*
power and property.
Nora probably felt the same
when a compañero approached her;
she began her timid *collaboration*
with the Frente Sandinista de Liberación Nacional.
Soon she exchanged readings
for meetings and transporting comrades.
Oscar Turcios taught her
within the limitations of her life experiences
until her need was synonymous
with the FSLN —
with the tortured peasants and students
and the exhausted petty bourgeoisie.
Then, too, she met Jorge Jenkins,
student FSLN rep,
and they promised political allegiance first
before their own vows.
She trusted his *higher level*
of political development.
Their engagement caused her father's heart arrest
but she married Jorge.
And slowly, again, she became isolated.
They moved to Italy
where he studied anthropology
and she, banking law and computers.
But isolation is more than geography or class.
I wonder if it was partly morning sickness,
the swollenness beyond expectation,
hunger for everything, anything, nothing —
even at the cost of one's vision.
You need him. You need

to protect the forthcoming —
first one daughter then another.
Or was the isolation *practical:*
when two have a meeting
the woman goes in principle.
But know that the woman
is there bathing the infants,
nursing, singing,
washing rice off the table and dishes
consumed by the house
with little to spare for politics
or oneself.
After five years
of what I've just imagined
Nora divorced her husband;
but, too, she separated from herself.
Was that it, Nora?
That queasy sensation
there's nothing under your feet.
So all you can think is
clutch the girls,
become active again or fall.
Meanwhile the number of executions
and disappeared
spread plague-like.
Then it was March 1978.
Nora, a lawyer for Nicaragua's
largest construction company,
met General Reynaldo Perez Vega,
the "Dog."
She contacted the compas.
They plotted.
Would she give up everything
(her daughters)
to kidnap him.
But she thought
part of my decision
was precisely because of my children.

So she invited over the General
who'd been waiting for her
to give it up for months.
He arrived within hours
giving her only enough time
to buy some liquor.
But he didn't want a drink
(*what for?* he asked);
he wanted the prize of his patience.
So she began the task:
unbuttoned his jacket,
slipped off his shirt gently
with an urgency akin to passion,
unbuckled his scarred belt,
pulled off his bruise-black boots.
Drawing his pants down
toward her lips
she spoke softly
a signal for her comrades.
They caved into the room like an earthquake
and held him down.
When she went out to tell his bodyguard
go buy us some rum
he couldn't hear the General's calls
above his car radio.
She returned to her bedroom
to find his throat slashed.
The "Dog" fought so intensely
there was no choice.
And it was *just as well*
she thought later
training in the mountains on the Northern Front.
She wondered what he would have done to her,
had done to many women
when promises weren't hot as a piece of ass
or when that wasn't it.
One less CIA agent, eh, Nora?
By June she was ready for combat

and became political leader
of four squadrons on the Southern Front.
Her eldest daughter, then six,
resented her disappearance.
If you had just told me, she said later.
For a mother who belongs to an organization
dedicated and poised to win
what can you say to your daughters.
Do the fathers leave
as if going to work as usual,
can they?
When does a woman know
what to say to her daughters.
Then, too, she was no longer
a corporate lawyer or mother or woman
though she was.
She was falling in love in the mountains
fighting beside her comrade
José María Alvarado.
She fought the National Guard
until six months pregnant
when they sent her to Costa Rica
in charge of financing the Southern Front.
I do not know what she was doing
July 19, 1979.
Perhaps in her last trimester
barely able to breathe
she shouted for the grandeur
of the peasants' Triumph.
Perhaps she wept, as I would.
And now with the war
directly against US intervention
she leads Nicaragua's mission to the UN—
where *Nora,* a male colleague admitted,
wears her past the way other women
wear perfume;
where, an opponent said,
Norita is a resonance box

and what is put into it
is decided in Managua.
Of course. That's her job.
Though no one would say that
of a man.
As I complete this narrative
I think of all the women
I'd love to fight alongside,
here, North of the Border,
as a gift to Nicaragua.

SEIZURE

In Nicaragua
old women
mobilize with sticks and boiling water
again.
You're North American.
You figure it's the season.
But back home
the moon
acts like that girl
who'd been fucked in so many places
she hardly knows which hole
is for babies
and you know you understand

un deber de cantar

and you know you understand
your desire
to see Broadway
NY NY
taken in a flash of July heat
and you know you want it.
(The green parrots snap
guapa
and your thighs sweat like mad.)
And you want it.
Shit. We don't have mountains here.
The rooftops
will do the trick

you think out loud.

Because you belong to a process
that belongs to you

one

you love to touch

and nurse

and deploy

on your lap, here,
Nicaragua. On your

lap, here Nueva
New York. Here

novio, baby

sister. When I say *mujeres*

man of course

I mean *y hombres*

también.
I'll never forget

the shower that riddled the tobacco fields
on the Honduran border of Nicaragua

where Suyapa
una niña de 4 años

learned June 9, 1983
what *somocistas* are

—*yanquis, contras*—
if she didn't know

before she was hit by mortar. Seizure
you envision

as the street
after the water has broken.

Note: *un deber de cantar,* "a duty to sing," is the title of a book by Rosario
Murillo, contemporary Nicaraguan poet.

RESISTANCE: A POEM ON IKAT CLOTH

By the time the forsythia blossomed
in waves along the parkway
the more delicate cherry and apple
had blown away, if you remember
correctly. Those were days
when you'd forget socks and books
after peeing in the privacy
of its branches and soft earth.
What a house you had
fit for turtles or sparrows.
One sparrow
wrapped in a silk kimono
wept for her tongue
clipped off by the old woman.
You'll never forget that
or its vengeance as striking
as the yellow around your small shoulders.
      shitakirisuzume mother called her.
      You didn't need to understand
      exactly.
a process of resistance
in Soemba, Sumatra, Java, Bali,
Timor,
      Soon came mounds of flesh
      and hair here and there.
      Centuries earlier
      you'd have been courted
or sold.
      "Inu has let out my sparrow — the little one
      that I kept in the clothes-basket she said,
      looking very unhappy."
For a Eurasian, sold.
      Murasaki
mother
      She soaked the cloth
      in incense
      then spread it on the floor
      standing there in bleached cotton,

red silk and bare feet.
And you fell in love with her
deeply as only a little girl could.
Pulling at your nipples
you dreamt of her body
that would become yours.
    "Since the day we first boarded the ship
    I have been unable to wear
    my dark red robe.
    That must not be done
    out of danger of attracting
    the god of the sea."
red as a Judy Chicago plate
feast your eyes on this
jack
    "when I was bathing along the shore
    scarcely screened by reeds
    I lifted my robe revealing my leg
    and more."
roll up that skirt
and show those calves
cause if that bitch thinks
she can steal your guy
she's crazy
    The cut burned
    so she flapped her wings
    and cried out
    but choked
    on blood.
The thread wound around your hand
so tight your fingers
turn indigo
    Murasaki
The Shining Prince realized
he could form her
into the one forbidden him. For that
he would persist
into old age.

                rice starch
envelope, bone, bride
                you can't resist
The box of the sparrow's vengeance
contained evils comparable to agent orange
or the minamata disease. The old man
lived happily
without the old woman. But why her?
except that she was archetypal.
                She depended on her child
                to the point that when her daughter died
                and she left Tosa
                she could only lie down
                on the boat's floor
                and sob loudly
                while the waves
                crashed against her side
                almost pleasantly.
This depth lent the writer
the soft black silt
on the ocean floor
where all life, some men say, began.
                warp
"Mr. Ramsay, stumbling along a passage
one dark morning, stretched his arms out,
but Mrs. Ramsay, having died rather suddenly
the night before, his arms though stretched out,
remained empty."
                when the men wove and women dyed
mother —
                mutha
Orchids you explained
represent female genitalia
in Chinese verse.
Hence the orchid boat.
Patricia liked that
and would use it in her collection
Sex and Weather.

the supremes soothed like an older sister
rubbing your back
kissing your neck and pulling you into
motor city, usa
whether you liked it
or not that
was the summer
of watts and though you
were in a coma
as far as that
the ramifications
the ramifications
bled through transistors
        a *class* act
blues from indigo, reds
from mendoekoe root, yellows, boiling
tegaran wood
and sometimes by mudbath
        when you saw her bathing in the dark
        you wanted to dip your hand in
mamagoto suruno?
        The bride transforms
        into water
        while the groom moves
        like the carp
        there just under the bridge —
        like the boy with you
        under the forsythia
        scratching and rolling around.
        No, actually you just lay there
        still and moist.
        Wondering what next.
pine
        You're not even certain
        which you see —
        the carp or the reflection of your hand.
the forsythia curled
like cupped hands covering

bound and unbound
As if blood
    "The thought of the white linen
    spread out on the deep snow
    the cloth and the snow
    glowing scarlet was enough
    to make him feel that"
The sight of him squeezing melons
sniffing one
then splitting it open in the park
was enough to make you feel that
    Naha, Ryukyu Island, Taketome, Shiga,
    Karayoshi, Tottori, Izo,
resistance does not mean
not drawn it means
    sasou mizu araba
    inamu to zo omou
bind the thread
with hemp or banana leaves
before soaking it in the indigo
black as squid as seaweed as his hair
    as his hair
    as I lick his genitals
    first taking one side
    deep in my mouth then the other
    till he cries softly
    please
for days
    Though practical
    you hate annotations
    to the *kokinshu;*
    each note vivisects
    a *waka*
    like so many petals
    off a stem
    until your lap
    is full of blossoms.
    How many you destroyed!

You can't imagine
Komachi's world
as real. Hair
so heavy it adds
another layer of brocade
(black on wisteria,
plum—)
forsythia too raw
　　　and the smell
　　　of fresh *tatami*.
　　　But can you do without
　　　kono yumei no naka ni
Can you pull apart the line
"my heart chars"
　　　kokoro yakeori
corridors of thread
　　　"creating the pattern from memory
　　　conforming to a certain style
　　　typical of each island"
"K.8. Fragment of ramie kasuri, medium
blue, with repeating double ikat, and mantled
turtles and maple leaves of weft ikat.
Omi Province, Shiga Prefecture,
Honshu.
L. 16.5 cm. W. 19.5 cm."
　　　"the turtle with strands of seaweed
　　　growing from its back forming a mantle,
　　　reputed to live for centuries,"
Komachi also moved
like those shadows in the shallows
you cannot reach
though they touch you.
Wading and feeling
something light as a curtain
around your calves you turn
to see very small scallops
rise to the surface
for a moment of oxygen

then close up and descend.
Caught, you look
at what he calls their eyes
(ridges of blue)
and are afraid to touch
that part.
          from memory or history
sasou mizu
          Grandmother's *ofuro*
          contained giant squid
killer whales
          hot
omou
          You were afraid he would
          turn to the sea
          to say something
          that would separate you
          forever
          so kept talking.
          Of course he grew irritable
          and didn't really want
          a basket of shells
          for the bathroom.
"his arms though stretched out"
          The line shocked you
          like so much of Kawabata
          who you blame
          for years of humiliation,
          katakana, hiragana, kanji,
at each stroke
          You first hear the squall
          coming across the lake
          like a sheet of glass.
          You start to cry and daddy
          rows toward the shore and mother.
in the Malayan Archipelago
          Georgia O'Keeffe's orchid shocked you
          so even now you can picture the fragrance

"Should a stranger witness the performance
he is compelled to dip his finger
into the dye and taste it. Those employed
must never mention the names of dead people
or animals. Pregnant or sick women
are not allowed to look on;
should this happen they are punished
as strangers."
   in the Malayan Archipelago
   where boys give their sweethearts
   shuttles they will carve, burn,
   name,
"language does not differ
from instruments of production,
from machines, let us say,"
   knocked down
knocked *up girl*
   "the superstructure"
he wouldn't stop talking
about *deep structure*
   and mention in prayer
but you need more than the female persona.
A swatch of cloth.
A pressed flower. The taste of powder
brushed against your lips.
   pine
matsu
   The wedding day chosen
   he brought you animal crackers
cloths
   Pushing aside the branches
   you crawl in
   on your hands and knees,
   lie back,
   and light up.
tabako chodai
   because the forsythia
   symbolizes so much

66

            of sneakers,
            cloth ABC books, charms,
sankyu
                  the "charred heart"
                  would be reconstructed thus:
"Before the golden, gentle Buddha, I will lay
Poems as my flowers,
Entering in the Way,
Entering in the Way."
                  fuck that shit
Link the sections
with fragrance: *matsu*
                  shards of ice
The bride spread out her dress
for the dry cleaners
then picked kernels of rice
off the quilt and from her hair.
                  bits of china
the lining unfolds
out of the body
through hormonal revolutions
gravity and chance
                  lick that plate clean
can I get a cigarette
                  got a match
click clack, click
clack
            chodai
in this dream
                  She wrapped the ikat
                  around her waist and set out
                  for Hausa, Yoruba, Ewe of Ghana,
                  Baule, Madagascar, and Northern Edo
I pull off my dress
and take a deep breath.
The cupped hands open then
onto the loom.
            click clack click

clack
and in the rhythmic chore
I imagine a daughter in my lap
who I will never give away
but see off
with a bundle of cloths
dyed with resistance

Ikat: "the technique of resist-dying yarn before it is woven" (African Textiles, John Picton and John Mack, London, 1979).

Line 11	Sparrow references from the Japanese folk tale, *"Shitakirisuzume"* (literally, "the tongue-cut-sparrow"). The sparrow received the punishment after eating the old woman's rice starch. The sparrow got even.
Line 22	Locations in Indonesia known for ikat.
Line 29	*Genjimonogatari (The Tale of Genji* by Murasaki Shikibu, translated by Arthur Waley). This is the first time Genji hears the child Murasaki who he later adopts, then marries.
Line 33	*Murasaki* also means "purple."
Line 45 & 54	*Tosanikki (The Tosa Diary* by Ki no Tsurayuki translated by Earl Miner), written in the female persona.
Line 72	"The Shining Prince" refers to Genji.
Line 100	*To the Lighthouse,* Virginia Woolf.
Line 129	Colors refer to dyes used in Indonesia. *(Ikat Technique,* Charles Ikle, New York, 1934).
Line 135	*Mamagoto suruno,* Japanese, "playing house."
Line 155	*Yukiguni (Snow Country,* Kawabata Yasunari, translated by Edward Seidensticker).
Line 164	Locations in Japan known for ikat.
Line 168	*Sasou* etc. is a quote from a waka (classical Japanese poem) by Ono no Komachi. Donald Keene translated these lines, "were there water to entice me/ I would follow it, I think." (*Anthology of Japanese Literature,* p. 79).
Line 183	*Kokinshu* is the Imperial Anthology of poetry completed in 905.
Line 200	*Tatami,* straw matting for the floor in Japanese homes.

Line 202	*Kono* etc., Japanese, for "in this dream."
Line 204-5	From another Ono no Komachi poem translated by Earl Miner *(Introduction to Japanese Court Poetry,* p. 82).
Line 207	Ikle, p. 50.
Lines 210-18	*Japanese Country Textiles,* Toronto, 1965, p. 16; p. 15.
Line 237	*Ofuro,* Japanese bathtub.
Line 257	*Katakana* etc. are the Japanese syllabaries and the Chinese characters respectively.
Line 267	Ikle, p. 51.
Line 279	Joseph Stalin, *Marxism and the Problems of Linguistics.*
Line 293	*Matsu,* Japanese, "pine tree" and "wait."
Line 302	*Tabako chodai,* Japanese, "give me a cigarette [tobacco]."
Line 307	*Sankyu,* Japanese pronunciation of "thank you."
Line 310	Noh play by Kan'ami Kiyotsugu, "Sotoba Komachi," supposedly about Ono no Komachi's repentance. (Keene, p. 270.)
Line 336	Locations in Africa known for ikat.

ACP3568   5/9/94